HARPER BLESSINGS

WITHDRAWN

 angels

 light

 bed

 moon

 cricket

 pray

 eyes

 sheep

 head

 stars

 heart

sun

 house

 window

HARPER BLESSINGS

Bedtime
Prayers

Edited by Jennifer Frantz

Illustrated by Renée Graef

HarperFestival®

A Division of HarperCollins*Publishers*

GOD BLESS THE MOON

I see the 🌙 ,

And the 🌙 sees me.

God bless the 🌙 ,

And God bless me.

LORD, WATCH OVER ME

The has set.

The are bright.

The is shining

In the night.

Lord, watch over me, as I sleep,

Like the shepherd guards

His .

ANGELS SHINE LIKE
STARS AT NIGHT

 shine like  at night

Giving off God's glory and .

 listen when we

At the end of every day.

And  guard our

 and keep

Our families safe while we sleep.

NOW I LAY ME DOWN
TO SLEEP

Now I lay me down to sleep.

I pray the Lord my soul

To keep.

 watch me

Through the night.

Until I wake in morning .

FAMILY PRAYER

When Mom and Dad

Turn off the ,

And kiss my ,

I thank God for blessing me,

With such a special family.

Here in our and in

Heaven above,

God bless my family

With Your love.

BEDTIME PRAYER

As I go to ,

These things I .

Lord, fill my

With love each day.

And let me see things

Through your .

Please make me strong,

And kind, and wise.

ALL THROUGH THE NIGHT

The in the field

Have all gone to .

I lay down to sleep

And let dreams fill my .

I know that God

Keeps me safe in his 🫀 .

All through the night

'Til a new day's start.

CRICKET SONG

Crick-crick-crick.

Hear the song,

Under your

All night long.

Crick-crick-crick.

 praise Him as they call,

"Thank you, God,

For making us all!"

PRAISE THE LORD

When the morning

Greets the sky

Praise the Lord

As you open your  .

In the afternoon as you play

Praise the Lord for this great day.

At night when

Twinkle above

Praise the Lord for all his love!

LIGHT OF GOD'S LOVE

Even in the dark of night.

There's a

That shines so bright.

I know I'm guarded by God's love

And watching from above.